Comments from some of the colleges who have ... t

"I liked its ... ... brief answers which are neither cute nor condescending."
— Bryn Mawr College
Bryn Mawr, PA

"One of the better booklets on the subject — concise, informative, and easy to read."
— University of California
Irvine, CA

"Practical, concise, affirms what I've been telling students. Addresses the real problems of fear, motivation, and clinging to traditional methods."
— St. Bonaventure University
St. Bonaventure, NY

"Easy to understand and read, yet thorough enough to be comprehensive."
— Delaware Technical College
Wilmington, DE

"Excellent resource — one of the best I've seen!"
— Buena Vista College
Storm Lake, IA

"The book is clear, concise and to the point. Eliminates over-detailing; hits the main areas of job hunting."
— Tri-State University
Angola, IN

"...one of the most concise, helpful references to aid my work orientation teaching."
— Southeast Community College
Cumberland, KY

THE JOB HUNT

*A Concise Guide
To The Biggest Job
You'll Ever Have*

By Robert B. Nelson

TEN SPEED PRESS

*Dedicated to my Mother and Father
for their ongoing love and support.*

Copyright © 1986 by Robert B. Nelson

Originally published by Occasional Press
Eight printings (1981–83) by Pragmatic Publications

1⊜
TEN SPEED PRESS
P.O. Box 7123
Berkeley, California 94707

Library of Congress Cataloging-in-Publication Data:

Nelson, Robert B.
    The job hunt.

    1. Job hunting.   I. Title.
HF5382.7.N44   1986   650.1'4   85-27921
ISBN: 0-89815-160-0

Book Design by Nancy Austin
Cover Design by Brenton Beck

Printed in the United States of America

 3   4   5   —   90   89   88   87

Contents

Acknowledgements

To Doug Nelson and Dr. Charles Green, who helped me with my first job search; to Randy Jennings for turning a rough manuscript into a monograph; to all the placement professionals who made suggestions for improvements on the initial versions of this booklet; to the Waage's—Shirley, John, Hank, and Joel—who have helped extensively over the years with promotions and administration; to all the great folks at Ten Speed Press: Phil Wood, who agreed to publish this book after several rejections; George Young, who suggested an improved format; Nancy Austin, for design and layout; and everyone else there who makes working with them so enjoyable; and to all those job seekers that refuse to give up their dream of finding a job doing what they really want to do— thank you all!

Preface

A college degree used to be a ticket to a guaranteed job. Times have changed, and now finding a job can be difficult regardless of your qualifications. Unless you are independently wealthy or your family owns a business, it is something you will have to do sooner or later. The first job can be hard to find and in today's market the lack of a technical degree can make it harder still. I believe that you can not only find a job, but can find your ideal job . . . IF you know how to go about it.

This is a practical handbook for action. It shows, in as logical and concise a manner as possible, the route of a successful job-hunt. You will find that its Socratic style reads quickly, and will serve as a ready resource long after you have launched yourself in the career of your choice. Happy hunting!

BOB NELSON
January 1986

1 *Marketing Yourself*

What are the prospects for finding a job? Without a doubt, the number of entry-level jobs that don't require technical expertise of some type (accounting, engineering, computers, etc.) has drastically diminished within the last decade. Good jobs are still available to graduates with non-technical degrees, but those graduates have to be more skilled in job-hunting.

Isn't it hard to get a job with a general degree? If you think so, yes. That attitude will show through in all you do or say. But most organizations are run by people with non-technical degrees and most jobs demand skills that are developed in any educational program.

Most jobs seem to have such specific requirements. Most that you hear about, anyway. Usually what is more important than specific requirements are the skills of thinking, working with people, and interrelating concepts. These skills, if you can show you have them, will open more doors for you than any others.

What are selling points I may be overlooking? You can probably pick from this list:
- A broad and fresh perspective of the job
- An unbiased, non-political approach to thinking

- The ability to relate different concepts to each other
- The ability to solve problems and think critically
- A "learning" attitude and ability to adapt to change
- The skills of writing, researching, evaluating
- Energy, enthusiasm, interest, motivation, initiative
- Good work habits and communication skills
- Low cost compared to more experienced candidates

How do I market these abilities? Learn to sell yourself and make a good impression. Document your past accomplishments using your resume. Demonstrate your strengths through your present behavior. For example, show initiative by taking initiative, communication skills by effectively communicating, willingness to learn by asking effective questions, follow-through by following through!

How do I display these traits? By running a widespread, direct, personal campaign in which you demonstrate these non-technical assets. Put extra energy into preparation and follow-through; take actions and risks few others would attempt. Make your own rules as to what's appropriate in job hunting.

What else is crucial? Empathy with an employer's needs and problems (understanding his or her perspective) demonstrates how you can help and why you are the person in the best position to do so. Employers are only concerned with what the position could do for you and your career as a secondary and less important issue. Identifying with the employer's perspective is crucial to your successful job search.

How do you find out what their needs and problems are?
The best way to learn is to ask. Inside sources can help.
Alternative methods are to read between the lines as to why
they might need to hire someone: investigate relevant news
publications, question others who know the field or the
specific company, and then make a list of questions you'll
want to have answered as you begin talking with individuals.

Once I discover the needs, then what? Fit your needs into
theirs. Emphasize the elements in your background that
most closely match their needs. Try to build a case for how
your entire existence has led to precisely this opportunity,
whether that opportunity is an existing job opening or a
position that you hope the employer will create for you.

What could I try to get in the door? Part-time work until a
full-time position opens, assisting on a project, an internship,
contract or freelance work, or even volunteering. All of these
alternatives show determination and patience on your part.

What, overall, is essential to my successful marketing campaign? The key is having direction and showing that you
have it. DECIDING WHAT TO DO. Justifying and exploring that
objective with your RESUME and INFORMATIONAL INTERVIEWS.
Knowing how to SEARCH for openings, and how to INTERVIEW
once you find them. Knowing how to FOLLOW-UP after interviews. Learn these skills and you'll be set for a lifetime of
having the job you want. You'll have the ability to find
employment and thus never feel uneasy about marketing
yourself!

2 *Deciding What To Do*

I'm not sure what I should do. Most people have trouble identifying the job they want. This may be because they don't know enough about different professions to make a choice, they haven't devoted any thought to the subject, or perhaps they have too many alternatives open to them.

What job should I look for? You are the only one who could know. An open-ended approach to job-hunting in which you ask an employer "What do you have?" or "What do you think I should be?" is:

Weak—For every position that you'd be "willing to try" there are a dozen applicants who see it as their ideal job.

Dangerous—They might tell you, and you might find yourself wondering what happened when you're stuck in the wrong career 20 years from now.

You have to do some initial self-analysis on your own.

Self-analysis is hard for me to do. Everyone hates to be analyzed and to look at oneself is even harder. Nevertheless, this activity is essential to making the rest of the job hunt both more effective and easier. Without some thought, your objective will not be clear to you or to a potential employer, and it will be obvious that you need to further define your goals.

I keep procrastinating. This activity gets harder to do the longer you wait. Start. Do anything to break the ice and get going. It could be writing your initial feelings and thoughts on the worksheet provided on pages 7–14. Right now. Take three minutes. Perhaps decide on important factors related to what job you want, such as: where you want to live; how long you can go without working (both financially and emotionally); and whether or not you want to continue your education, and if so, how soon? The longer you delay answering these questions, the less time you'll have for the job-hunting steps that follow. Procrastinating will seriously impair your chances of getting the job you want.

I have no idea what I want to do. This is highly unlikely. Try listing those jobs you absolutely would not consider, or describe what you'd do if you could do anything—practicality and income requirements aside. Your ideal job. This should definitely be a written process. Writing allows you to be more objective, to add to the list at a later time, and to get a sense of progress in your efforts.

How else can I identify my ideal job? Investigate resources that list job descriptions and titles. Some of these resources are mentioned in the Appendix of this book. Take an inventory of your past and present experiences and interests:

What are characteristics of past work experiences that were positive?
What were your favorite courses? Activities? Why?
What are your strengths?
What are your "musts" and "wants" in a job?

What skills do you have and enjoy?

What do you daydream about?

How do you picture yourself in the future—5, 10, or even 20 years from now?

How do I decide between alternatives? If you have time, try each one. Trying might involve being an intern, doing volunteer work or even focusing a research project on the area of interest. If you don't have time to experience each alternative environment, the next best thing would be to accumulate as much information as possible about each. Talk to people in those professions. What are their likes and dislikes? The major problems and frustrations they encounter? What excites them most in their day-to-day work?

Do I have to know exactly what I want before I start looking? Absolutely not. Preferably your choice should be tentative and the job hunt should serve to confirm it. You want to be clear and precise about your selection criteria but the specific job—even if ideally identified—should be a general category. Your objective is to show that you've thought about all this and have a firm, yet open mind!

Can't I decide while I look? One would think so, but this rarely works. You've got to do some of the initial thinking on your own to come up with at least a general idea of what it is that you want to do. Once you have that foundation, you have a base to work from which can be revised as you learn more about the opportunities in your chosen field. This way you will be less influenced by the first opportunity that comes your way, and will seek (and hold out for) what you really want to do.

Analysis Worksheet

Which of your skills and abilities do you enjoy the most?

What are your primary interests and favorite pastimes?

What were your favorite college courses?

List some positive experiences you've had and the reasons you enjoyed each of them. What specific skills were you using?

What jobs do you daydream about? What do you see yourself doing in ten years?

What would your ideal job be like? Describe it from as many perspectives as possible. Visualize yourself in it. Who are you working with? How are you spending your time?

What are your criteria for selecting a position?

MUSTS

BENEFITS
CLOSER TO HOME
VARIETY IN DAY TO DAY WORK
STRONG COMPANY
RESPONSIBILITY
LEARNING
GROWTH POTENTIAL

WANTS

TUITION REIMB.
PEOPLE MY AGE,
INTERESTS TO
WORK WITH

What strengths and experiences most qualify you for your ideal job?

What gaps in your experience, knowledge or skills need to be overcome in order for you to achieve your ideal job or career?

If your ideal job is not readily achievable, what jobs could you take now that would lead you in the right direction or get you into the appropriate environment?

To whom could you talk to obtain more information useful to your career planning?

1)

2)

3)

4)

5)

On what other activities must you work to prepare for job-hunting, and for your career?

   ACTIVITY   *COMPLETE BY*

What are your immediate and long-term career objectives based upon your analysis?

3 *The Resume*

What is the purpose of a resume? To obtain an interview. This can be quite a challenge since the average resume receives only 5–7 seconds of viewing. No one is ever hired solely on the basis of how they look on paper. The resume is your promotional literature for selling yourself. It serves to whet an employer's appetite and make him or her want to know more about you.

How do I accomplish that purpose? By providing the most relevant information in as concise a manner as possible: the most positive, impressive highlights from your past that would be applicable to the position you seek. Understand and answer the question from the employer's perspective: Does this applicant come close to matching any of our current or forthcoming needs?

What's a good way to start? Describing yourself on paper is difficult and somewhat dehumanizing. One method is to randomly list information about yourself, set it aside and add to it later. Place the accumulated data in a format that best emphasizes your strengths and then delete the least relevant information. A critique by another person can also be of help.

What's important to emphasize? In order of importance, (1) experience relevant to the job you are seeking, (2) your most recent experience, and (3) experience extending over a long period. Focus on what you have achieved and learned and not just on how and where you have spent your time. Be as specific as possible in citing examples to support your statements, using numbers, percentages, and timeframes whenever possible. Consider responsibilities from as many employer angles as possible, such as: budget responsibility, customer contact, advancement and level of authority.

I'm having trouble narrowing down information. A resume is not a biography. It should emphasize only your very best side, using information most applicable to the job opportunity at hand. Regardless of the amount of time you spent on a particular job, or how important you thought it was, use only the most impressive tip of the iceberg that also relates to the employer's needs.

It's still hard to cut out information. Editing is difficult, but essential; without editing, the most relevant information might get buried. You can't just try to squeeze things in or use smaller type. Less is more: less information, more impact. To put in everything, hoping to miss nothing, does not work!

I feel like I'm bragging. There's no room for modesty on a resume. Employers expect to see ideal candidates, and those who don't portray themselves as such are seldom given the benefit of the doubt. Many of the items listed on resumes are exaggerated if not outright lies. Don't lie, but don't sell yourself short. Save being humble for the interview.

Is tone important in a resume? Tone is the personality that comes through in a resume, from the sentence structure, word selection, number of verbs, etc. It can say as much about you as the content. For example, a resume that has a business tone will convey a directness and a sense of urgency in word and sentence structure: short sentences, appropriate jargon, and active rather than passive words.

"What's a statement of objective"? This sentence or two located at the beginning of your resume or in your cover letter that tells a prospective employer at a glance if you are a possible match for any employment needs. It is both general, so as to not exclude you from openings you might want to be considered for, yet specific, so it communicates some boundaries to the employer. It is essential for individuals who have extensive unrelated experience. Some examples:

- An entry-level position in marketing or sales support for a manufacturing firm.
- An administrative position for a small or medium-sized non-profit organization.
- A research assistant for a professor or service organization.

What if all of my experience is unrelated to my objective? You might want to summarize the various skills you have learned in past jobs. Then simply list the position titles and places in one section of the resume. This format, known as a "functional" resume, focuses attention on the skills most relevant to your objective.

What should not be included in a resume? Information unrelated to your job objective. A picture, your height and weight, Social Security number, hobbies, information inappropriate to the position at hand, misspelled words, long words from a dictionary to impress someone, any ambiguous information (either simplify or eliminate), slang or jargon words or phrases, abbreviations or slashes. Avoid flowery adjectives and overused phrases, as well.

How creative should I be? Although you should want your resume to stand out from the masses, this should be achieved more through content and less through format. The resume serves the functional purpose of explaining why you are qualified for a position.

What else do I need to know? Standard length for a resume is one page; a longer resume indicates you're trying to say too much or are stuck on yourself. It never hurts to have it typeset or use heavier or toned paper. Avoid the use of "I" since this is assumed. You should use different resumes for different job categories, with the information slanted accordingly. There are no magic words that always sound good. What looks good on another resume may detract from your resume. It's important to be sincere and appropriate, citing relevant information and statistics to support your claims.

Where do I distribute the resume? Have the resume ready to send to all individuals you contact. It can also be attached to any application you will complete to present your qualifications in a format that you have control over.

What do I send with my resume? A personal letter of introduction, or cover letter, should always accompany your resume. It serves to arouse the potential employer's interest in you and your resume, and briefly explains your qualifications and why you are sending the resume.

To whom should the letter and resume be sent? This information should always be sent to the person you have spoken with who has the authority to hire you. Always confirm the spellings of names and the accuracy of titles in advance.

Is there a format to the cover letter? You can be a little more creative here than with the resume. A good cover letter will contain:

AN ATTENTION GRABBER—an impressive bit of information about you or what you could do for the firm, if hired. Present an incentive for them to be interested in you.

RESUME HIGHLIGHTS—a few impressive facts elaborated upon in the body of your resume.

ACTION—what you intend to do as a follow-up to the resume. Never request action of a potential employer; you should be taking the initiative and not cause him or her extra work.

What else? Cover letters should be individually typed, addressed to a person with whom you have spoken, and personally signed. The length should be 2–3 paragraphs.

Standard Cover Letter

Your address

Date spelled out

Full name of employer
Title of employer
Organization name spelled out
Address

Dear Mr. or Ms. Last Name: ◀ *Attention getter*

Reference your recent telephone conversation
with the individual or how else you came to be
writing him or her. State a remarkable fact or
qualification about yourself. Explain your area
of interest or purpose in writing.

◀ *Transition to resume highlights*

Explain how your interests, abilities and experience would fit into the career or position you
seek. Distinguish yourself from other candidates by emphasizing specific qualifications.
Lead the reader into the enclosed resume by
mentioning one or two of the most relevant items
on the resume.

◀ *Intended action or follow-up*

Thank the individual and explain what you will
do next to follow-up on the letter. If a meeting
is already scheduled, confirm the time and place.

Sincerely,

Your full name signed
Your full name typed

Enclosure

★ *P.S.: See sample cover letters on pages 63-64.*

Standard Resume

NAME

Current address   Permanent address
street, state, zip code   (only if you plan to move
phone number   during your job search)

◄ *Put your objective here or in your cover letter.*

PROFESSIONAL OBJECTIVE

This tells an employer at a glance if you'd be interested in the opening at hand. Immediate or career objectives, or both, are indicated. Because it is assumed, avoid saying "a challenging and demanding position in . . ."

◄ *Place this section next if you are just graduating from an educational program.*

EDUCATION

Your college, its location, dates attended (spelled out) B.A. (or B.A. candidate), graduation date. Major/Minor. Additional marketable coursework such as computer languages or statstics that could apply to the job, the profession, or to business in general. Also, honor societies, an honors thesis, or special educational experiences such as international study programs.

EXPERIENCE

● *Keep a consistent format!*

Title of Position, Name of Institution, location, dates employed Don't bury this category, even if it doesn't look impressive for the job you seek. Employers don't expect a new graduate to have extensive experience, but do want an indicator of your ability to work and hold a job. Three or four entries should be sufficient. List volunteer positions, internships and unusual experiences as regular jobs if they relate to the position sought. The more dated the experience, the less significance it is likely to have. Be selective in choosing the experiences most relevant to the job you seek.

Title of Position, Name of Institution, location, dates employed
The format can vary as long as it is consistent from position
to position. Whatever format you use should make your
strengths stand out. If you use a chronological format, list
your most recent experience first. A functional format would
place your most relevant experience first.

RELATED ACTIVITIES
List here anything else that might relate in a positive way to
the job sought: examples of leadership, professional interests,
and additional skills.

Month 198__

Your resume should fit on one
8½" × 11" page.

★ P.S.: See additional resumes
on pages 70–81

Additional Resume Tips

Be Specific

- Trained three new employees.
- Decreased errors by 15 percent saving over $4000 in one year.

- Learned new procedures in a record two weeks.

Not Vague

- Did some training.

- Helped reduce errors.

- Was a fast learner.

Be Active & Direct

- Completed . . .

- Used resources effectively.

- Was responsible for . . .

Not Passive & Wordy

- Was in charge of completion of . . .

- Made utilization of the following resources:

- Had the responsibility for . . .

Be Positive

- Assisted customers with. . .

- Improved product potential . . .

- Made a career move to . . .

Not Negative

- Handled complaints of . . .

- Avoided loss of market share . . .

- Was laid off from . . .

Focus on Achievements	*Not Time & Activities*
• Was promoted and received two merit increases.	• Worked there three years.
• Completed all projects on schedule.	• Handled odd jobs.
• Successfully handled supervisory responsibilities.	• Filled in for the assistant manager.

Resume Worksheet

Objective:

Education:

Experience:

Related Activities:

★ Try a rough sheet set up like this, or one page for each item.

4 Informational Interviewing

What is informational interviewing? It's an activity that allows you to (1) clarify your thoughts about your career plans while you (2) learn more about different professions or areas of the same profession, and (3) most importantly, get inside organizations and talk directly to those individuals who could hire you.

Why should I do it? Because if it's done well, it yields a non-threatening dialogue between you and potential employers in which you can obtain useful information that will lead to job offers. It's a comfortable way to start your job searching.

I'm not interested in talking . . . I want a job! Although this activity seems off-the-track of your goal of obtaining a job, it is usually the best approach for eventually securing employment.

Will managers take time to talk with me? If surveyed they would probably indicate that they do not have the time for such an activity. In practice, however, they usually enjoy discussing themselves, their profession, and their organization with others who indicate an interest in such things. It also gives them a chance to reflect upon their constantly changing needs and circumstances.

How do I arrange a meeting? Call the head of the department or the manager in the area of your interest who has the authority to hire you. Ask for some time for the purpose of investigating a field of work, the industry, or their particular company or department. Remember, that person initially does not know who is on the other end of the telephone ... you may be a friend or relative of the president of the company, or perhaps the next largest customer the company will have. You'll typically be given the benefit of the doubt.

What do I talk about? Either on the telephone or in a meeting, if possible, you should have questions prepared about the industry, its future, who the competition is, how markets are developed, product and service distribution methods and areas of growth. Avoid directly mentioning that you are looking for a job early in the conversation. Instead, try to learn about the company and the industry.

Then what? Once you've met the person, express interest in all you see and hear. Ask for a tour. Learn as much as possible about your field of interest and options available to you. Try to make a friend. Don't ask for a job. This is one of the few occasions in your life when you can randomly talk with individuals about things that interest you. Enjoy it.

How do I change the subject to employment considerations? There should be a natural shift in the conversation after you have many of your questions answered, so that you will have a chance to talk about yourself and your future. Explain that you are interested in the profession and hope to enter it soon. Ask about upcoming opportunities within the department. Don't be anxious to say that you are currently looking for a position. If you have made a favorable impression employers will often suggest that you consider their company for employment. At the very least, you will have learned from each question that was answered, and will thus become a more informed prospect.

I feel awkward bringing up the topic of employment. Then don't. If it seems as though you might misrepresent your intentions in meeting with the individual, do not mention the topic. Instead, call the individual back three to four weeks later and say that after extensive thought you are now committed to the profession that was discussed, are impressed with that particular company, and ask if he or she is aware of any opportunities within the firm.

Isn't this a lot of effort for one job? Yes, but very little for one career, a potential lifetime of contacts, and a better knowledge of the pros and cons of a field in which you have not yet worked.

5 *Searching*

How do I start searching? If you did any informational interviewing, you already have. You've gained practice in interviewing and have developed a network of contacts to develop further.

What process should I follow? You want to get the word out that you are available. Do this in a personal, direct manner by calling 50-75 individuals in your area of interest and asking them about their company and upcoming opportunities. Talk to anyone who will talk to you. Leave no stone unturned.

Why can't I just apply for a few jobs at a time? You can, but your chances of success are less with such a limited approach. Try it if you want to (you may get lucky!), but set a time limit for yourself (two to three weeks), and revise your approach if unsuccessful after that period of time.

Where do I get 50-75 leads? Ask each person you contact for additional names and resources. In order of probable value, you might want to also check with:

Your academic advisor
College professors

List from Career Expo

Anyone in your field of interest

Alumni volunteers from your college placement office

Alumni in your profession (from your alumni association)

Friends and friends of friends

Parents and parents' friends

Professional associations — AMA

Community groups with whom you are involved

Career planning and placement libraries — school

The Yellow Pages of the phone book

Listings of area employers

Chambers of commerce

Industrial directories

Newspaper ads (recent and past)

Personnel offices

Employment agencies (fees paid by employer only)

Who will hire me? An employer will hire you if you can convince him or her that you can contribute toward achieving the employer's goals. Try to lower the employer's risk in taking a chance on you. In other words: what you can do and how good you are at proving it determines who will offer you a job.

I just want a job until I figure out what to do. This is a viable alternative, but be careful about being stereotyped or pigeon-holed in ways that could preclude future opportunities. It is easy to become comfortable and put off those real decisions while staying busy.

What do I say to people I don't know when I call them for the first time? Try a variation on one of the following: "Hi,

Mr. Smith. My name is … I'm graduating from Podunk University in May of this year, with a degree in…. I wanted to find out about the services and products your business provides. Do you have a few minutes to talk?" or "I'm trying to clarify my career interests. Who could be the best person in your organization for me to talk to regarding what your company does and what opportunities might be upcoming?" Most people are willing to talk at least a few minutes about themselves and what they do.

Why not just ask if they're hiring? You can do this, but it usually is too blunt an approach. Such a point-blank question will yield a "yes" ("please send your resume") or a "no" (end of the conversation). Either way you haven't learned any more about the employer, the position, or the profession, and your chances of being considered for employment remain small.

What if a secretary answers? If you wish to speak to a specific person, ask for him or her by name. If the person is not there, ask when might be a good time to call again. Try not to leave a message if the person you are calling does not know who you are. If you do not have a name to ask for, ask "who is the appropriate person to speak to about the products and services of (company name)?" or "Who is the manager in charge of the Graphics Department (or other areas of the firm which relate to your career interests)?"

Then what do I do? Learn from them. Ask about their products and services. Ask their advice. Ask if you may send a resume, even if they don't have any openings. Seek additional names and resources. Ask who else is hiring. Thank them for assisting.

What else do I need to know? Take good notes and develop a good system of recording information. Indicate the times and dates of telephone calls you made and responses you received.

What are the less likely places to look? SEARCH FIRMS are infrequently used by employers for entry-level positions. NEWSPAPER ADS are also a last resort for most employers. Often jobs for which a non-technical degree would qualify have numerous candidates from "walk-ins" and filed resumes. PERSONNEL DEPARTMENTS should also be avoided as an initial resource. These are all secondary sources. Go instead to primary sources, that is, individuals who can directly hire you.

Are there any lists I can get on? Not many, and if you did it would inevitably be with thousands of similar applicants. It is much more advantageous to be the only candidate.

How is that possible? Ideally, you want to talk with employers before they have positions officially open. Once an opening is announced, you are more likely to become just another face in the crowd of applicants. Find employers who have forthcoming needs that are not yet widely advertised or clarified, or even by having a position created for you.

How do I do that? It goes back to running an aggressive campaign to market yourself. Often one thing leads to another so that someone with whom you are talking says: "You know, we normally don't do this, but . . ." or "I bet that Smith could really use someone like you on that new project. Let me give her a call."

It still sounds like a long shot. The search gets shorter the more places you look and the more leads you follow. A "networking" approach is much more effective than the typical haphazard approach.

What is the typical approach? The typical job-searching approach, which is responsible for more failures than any other mistake made in the job-hunting process: (1) following only a few leads at a time. One lead pursued with excitement and anticipation; waiting for an interview or response; being rejected and taking it personally; becoming depressed and waiting before you look again (wasting time); repeating this cycle over and over until you are emotionally drained and mentally stagnant. Two or three rejections will dampen your spirit and being to erode your attitude; five or more rejections can put you into a serious slump that might take months to turn around; (2) seeking only "secondary" sources that are second- or third-hand, e.g., want ads, placement agencies, personnel, etc. Such sources often list opportunities that are out of date and usually have extensive competition; and (3) approaching leads impersonally, e.g., by writing letters only (without calling first), and sending those letters to companies in care of departments instead of to specific individuals.

What is the networking approach? This approach involves: 1) pursuing 50 to 75 leads, matter-of-factly processing them; constantly looking for additional contacts and asking for referrals; keeping busy while waiting for responses; accepting rejection (their loss); 2) going mainly to "primary" sources, i.e., those individuals who have the authority to hire you; and 3) approaching individuals in a personal and professional manner — on the phone or, if possible, in person. This should result in a higher percentage of interviews, a high percentage of job offers, a choice of jobs, and most importantly, a positive prevailing attitude. This approach can be the most important factor in a successful job campaign! The key is how you START. Start big, end big.

Why don't more people use the approach that works? For one of three reasons: 1) They lack motivation. Job hunting is not important enough to them to want to do it right. They don't want to put in the time and effort that is required to get the job they want. 2) They lack knowledge. No one ever told them the "right" way to find a job and they've relied on "common knowledge" approaches (e.g., checking the want ads) that are ineffective. They haven't known where to find potential job contacts and how to approach those individuals. 3) They lack skills. They know what they should do, but they are unable to do it. Perhaps they lack interpersonal communication skills, the ability to manage their time, or the ability to organize their job search—all skills which can easily be acquired with practice.

Is attitude important? It is essential, especially when your abilities are unknown and your experience is limited. Attitudes represented by initiative, enthusiasm, motivation, confidence and energy go a long way.

Sounds like a full-time effort. If you want to do it right, it is. A small sacrifice if a professional job is important to you. At the very least, be ready to put forth an all-out effort when you will have the time—during vacation breaks, for instance. Have a resume drafted, start a list of leads, and be ready to go. Plan on taking 30 to 90 days.

Sounds like a game. Right again. Make it fun. Also recognize that there are formal and informal games.

What is the formal game? This involves doing all the "right" things, even though they may have little chance of netting you a job. Applications, resumes, personnel departments are all part of the traditional process.

Should I avoid personnel departments? No. Just don't limit yourself to using them as your only method of searching. Likewise with classified ads.

What is the informal game? The one that really determines who is selected for jobs. Besides specific qualifications, it involves the right people liking you, lucky timing, setting your own rules, persistence and creativity.

Why even bother with the formal game? Because although it may not get you a job, not playing it can prevent you from getting one. It is necessary to play both games.

How do I get people to like me? You can answer that easily with what works for you. Show interest in others and in their activities, be considerate and polite, flexible and grateful.

What if I become discouraged? Join the crowd. It's bound to happen. Just make sure that you do not keep making the same mistakes. Keep plugging, but BE SURE YOU ARE DOING THE RIGHT THINGS. Make it fun; this is one of the few times in your life that you will be able to call people at random and talk about those things that most interest you.

How do I handle rejection? Don't dwell on it. Keep busy developing options, and opportunities which fall through will be easier to overcome. Redirect your frustrations into productive energy by expanding your searching efforts.

A final note . . . Be careful not to exclude options or leads too soon. Even if you don't think you would like a particular job you've heard about, you can always refuse it after you have obtained an offer. The practice you'll receive in going through the entire process will be invaluable in fine-tuning your job-hunting skills for that one opportunity that you really want.

Searching Worksheet

Current leads:

People who could give me additional leads:

Other sources to check for contacts:

Telephone Calling Worksheet

Introduction (name, brief sales pitch and specific question):

Your next statement if it is not the appropriate person:

Your next statement if it is the appropriate person (that is, the person who could hire you):

"Rapport" questions (general, open-ended, non-threatening):
    What does your department do?
    Who do you serve? How do you market your services?
    What are the main concerns of your department?
    How does one typically enter your profession?
    Are there others whom you'd suggest I contact?
    Is it all right if I send you my resume? I'm interested in
        your comments.
    Other questions:

Key information-seeking questions (specific, yielding impor-tant information for your search—use if the conversation flows well):

What problems or needs do you currently have?

What are your greatest frustrations on the job?

How did you attain your position?

What areas of your company are growing fastest?

What advice would you give someone starting out?

What employment needs do you have now or foresee in the near future?

Other questions:

6 *Interviewing*

What is the objective of an interview? For the employer, it is to see if your paper image and portrayal stand up in real life: to see if you are a "match" for the position at hand. Your objective should be to explore whether or not this is a place you'd like to work. Formulate open-ended questions and probe. Look for indicators. Ideally, you should be interviewing to obtain as many offers as possible, so that you have a choice between offers.

Do I have to dress up? Yes, although more formal dress is usually most appropriate, you want to gear yourself to the dress standards of the workplace. When in doubt, dress up to show you take the interview seriously.

How do I make an impression? Don't try to be anyone but yourself. Smile. Use a firm handshake and frequent eye contact. Elaborate on information from your resume that indicates you will work out well, that the risk in hiring you is small, and that you have a steady, predictable record of dedication to those things that are important to you. Be confident yet modest.

What should I bring? Anything that can support your case, but don't bring items to light until the appropriate time in the flow of conversation. A few well-placed examples of your work are far more effective than proving you have skills that may not be necessary for this particular job. You don't want to seem overbearing.

What is the best way to prepare? You must have a good understanding of your abilities as they relate to the job you are applying for. You can do this simply: (1) List all of the questions that you think you'll be asked. (See sample questions, pages 45–46. (2) Talk to someone in the field, in a similar position, or someone who is knowledgeable about interviewing. (3) Role-play the interview with a friend, roommate, or fellow job-hunter.

How do I get information about the position? Many firms are willing to send you a job description if you ask for one. It is possible to get a wealth of information about companies and even some individuals from a library. Your college placement office has brochures, annual reports and related information.

How do I get information during an interview? You will always be given a chance to ask questions. Remember, though, that good interviewers will control the interview so that they first get all of the information they want about you before they tell you too much about the job. In this way they avoid "telegraphing" the right answers to their questions.

What do you mean by "telegraphing"? Giving the best answers to their questions. For example, "This job requires good communication skills. How are your communications skills?" Obviously you would know to reply that your communication skills are strong.

How can I get them talking first? After you answer a question, ask a question. This will tend to make your interview more conversational and natural. Ask open-ended questions that can't be answered with a "yes" or "no." For example, in what direction is the company moving? How would a typical day on the job be spent? What training opportunities exist? Ask about the interviewer. How did he or she join the company? What does he or she like best about working for the company?

What other techniques might the interviewer use? If the interviewer has been trained in interviewing, he or she might "funnel" questions from the general to the specific. This is a way to get the interviewee to walk through a situation as if it were actually happening. For example: "Did you deal with customers on your last job?" "Did you ever deal with a negative customer?" "How did you handle that person?" "What if they still didn't respond to your approach?" "And if that didn't work?" This is a way to find out what you were thinking while you were in that situation.

What questions will most likely be asked? You can guess a lot of them. The questions will focus on how you could meet their needs. The employer might ask about gaps or ambiguous information on your resume. Some other questions to expect include: Why do you want this job? What will you do you don't get it? If you're interested in business (government, education, etc.) why did you major in history (English, sociology, philosophy, etc.)? ("I took history to improve my verbal skills, to learn how to research problems, and to analyze leadership theories of yesteryear.") Will you relocate? (Will you really?) When are you available? Will you be willing to wait two months for this position? Three months? Six months? Do you plan to go to graduate school? ("Possibly, but I want to obtain some work experience first.") What salary do you expect? ("Competitive or appropriate to my experience and potential.") See the list on page 45 for additional questions.

What are the unspoken questions? Will this person fit the job? The group? Can I justify hiring this person? Will the value outweigh the cost of hiring this applicant? Will he or she accept the position if it is offered? Does the applicant really want the job?

How honest should I be? Be honest, but not blunt. Don't offer negative information that is unnecessary. At the same time, you'll fit in best if you leave no surprises, especially about your abilities. Answer the questions asked.

What if I am asked a question I can't answer? You more than likely will not be quizzed during your interview. A question that throws you can be handled by asking for clarification or for an example. If you don't know, say so, but too many of these replies may indicate that you did not prepare enough for the interview.

Will I be asked any trick questions? Maybe. They will probably be concerned with how serious you are about this career, profession and job. A typical question might be: "What other alternatives or positions are you considering?" You want it to appear as if you are hoping to receive a job offer from this company. "Well, since this is exactly what I'm looking for, I've postponed looking at other positions. If I'm not accepted, I would probably check with . . . (name their leading competitor)."

What should I ask about? Whatever is necessary to meet your criteria for selection, and to give you a good feel for the job, the people, and the working environment. Examples might include: What are the basic responsibilities of this position, and how much time will be spent on each? With whom will I be working? What are the major problems faced by this area of the company? How much travel, and of what duration, is expected? How much pressure might I encounter? What style of management prevails in this area or in the company? What's the next step in the selection process?

Any other advice? Try to project yourself into the job as much as possible. This is a way of looking past the offer and presuming an acceptance. Find out what you'd be doing the first day, week, and month of employment. Be able to explain how you would initially approach these responsibilities. If the interview has gone well, ask for the job while you're there.

Interviewing Questions

There is no way to be able to predict all of the possible questions you may be asked in an interview. The following questions have been taken from interview evaluation forms used by several different employers.

Why should I hire you?

What are your current job expectations?

Describe your educational background.

What was your favorite course in school? Why?

Describe the previous jobs you have had, beginning with your most recent.

What were your major responsibilities in your last job?

What are some of the things you did particularly well in your last job? (Or achieved the greatest success in?)

Why did you leave your last job?

Most jobs have positive and negative qualities. What were some of the negative qualities of your last job?

What did you like most/least about your past jobs/academic work?

Describe something you did that was not normally part of your job.

Do you like working with figures?

What do you think are the qualities of a good supervisor?

What do you consider to be the perfect job for you?

What do you feel have been your most significant accomplishments?

Give an accurate description of yourself.

Would you have any trouble making it to work by 8:00 a.m.?

Describe what you see as your major strengths and weaknesses for this position.

Are there certain things you feel more confident about doing? What are they, and why do you feel the way you do?

If you had a choice of responsibilities within this department which would you prefer?

How do you perceive your role in interacting with other department members?

What key factors attract you to this position or company?

What do you see yourself doing in five years?

How much independence and flexibility do you like in a job?

What do you expect for a starting salary?

When can you start?

Interviewing Worksheet

What gaps or ambiguous information appear on my resume?

What are my strongest assets in relation to this position?

What do I need to learn about the position, company or interviewer before the interview? How can I do that?

What should I take to the interview?

> *Additional resumes*
> *A list of references with telephone numbers*
> *Papers and projects*
> *Transcripts*
> *Letters of recommendation*
> *Four-year education plan (describing and tying your education to your future plans)*
> *Other:*

What are my selection criteria and what information do I need to know about the job, environment, or company?

7 *Follow-Up*

How important is the thank-you letter? Thank-you letters have been found to be the only correlation between people who are looking for positions and those who get hired. They've been found to correlate even more than qualifications, amount of experience, or even degree of interest.

What is involved in a good thank-you letter? This is usually personal, explaining your interest in the position (you could have changed your mind!), referring to a topic which was discussed, or providing more indicators of how well you'll fit in. More information about your qualifications, an example of your work, and alternative solutions to a problem which you learned of during the interview would all be appropriate. This letter serves to concisely remind the employer about you at the time of the employment decision.

When should I send it? Ideally, you want them to receive it when they are comparing applicants. Usually this takes place from several days to several weeks after your interview, depending upon how far along the selection process was.

Is timing important? Yes. Most job processes, including selections and applicant review, are RANDOM. The most qualified applicant is frequently buried beneath those who were a bit more aggressive and marketed themselves more effectively. Hence, the more leads you pursue, the greater your chances are of success. The final element in selection often tends to be the personality mix between you, your manager, and the work group.

Why is the personality mix so important? For the employer it is the difference between a team member and a headache. For you, it is probably the single most important element of a pleasant and successful first job. After all, you don't have extensive technical skills to make you invaluable in your job. You're still green.

How can I be persistent without being overbearing? Proper follow-up is more a matter of the right timing, not the quantity of contacts. Ask when the decision is being made, or check back when you feel your resume has been reviewed or the hiring decision is being made.

What should I do if I think I'm being stalled? Employers often put an applicant on hold. This may be because they are waiting for final approval of the position or because they think they can attract more qualified applicants if they delay. You can force the issue subtly by alluding to another job offer, or you can be more blatant by giving a date by which you need to know their decision. Either method indicates you have a sense of value and self-worth and are not willing to be put off. Be careful, though, not to appear too demanding.

I was rejected, but I have no idea why. Chances are small that you'll ever get the real reason. If you ask, you will be told the reason that you expect to hear. No one likes to argue with a rejected applicant. If, however, you felt that you did have a good chance, you should persist and acquire information that can help you for your next interview. The feedback as to how you came across is essential to keep you from working in a vacuum. Remember that the entire job-hunting process can be a learning experience, and the potential for learning is greatest with rejections.

How should I deal with rejection? Become busy when you start to feel low. The extra activity will generally carry you through until things get better. Take a break or try a change of pace for a day or two.

What else? If you get an offer, remember that it is on a contractual basis and get all your cards on the table. Do you plan to go home for three weeks within two months? Can you push for an early performance review or extra training? When can you expect a salary increase? Most important of all: be grateful and determined to succeed at the opportunity.

8 *After You Are Hired*

Come to closure with hanging leads. Contact any employers who are still considering you and tell them you've found a job; thank them for their interest. Regardless of the profession you choose, you can be certain that it is a tight network. You may want to work for one of those other employers later, or keep in contact with them in your current position.

Learn to listen. Effective listening is not an easy skill to master and apply. Pick up on others' priorities, hidden agendas, and unstated attitudes.

Learn the background of your area. The history of the people and recent changes in the department can help give you indicators about the "rules"—written and unwritten—in the area, and what changes to expect in the future.

Learn the informal power network. Bear in mind that power is often outside the formal structure. Who is respected and who is not? Who has the most influence and on what topics? Who has lunch with whom, or who stops for drinks after work? Whose OPINION of you is going to matter more than anything you do? Hard work alone is not necessarily the road to success . . .

Make time for the people as well as the task. An eager new graduate might easily focus too narrowly on doing a good job and ignore paying enough attention to developing good relationships with others at work. Both are important. Be sensitive to your place within the hierarchy. Although you may often see an easier or better way to do something, your employer will become frustrated if you appear more concerned with changing things than with learning how and why things are as they are. Focus on improving things AFTER you fully understand them.

Be sensitive to processes. What may seem slow or inefficient might serve a valuable purpose that is not initially apparent. Similarly, the ideas you have may not be as important as the way you present them. There is a right time, method and place for all communication. Learn proper timing through observing others who are effective in the workplace.

Keep the right attitude and perspective. Be appreciative of the opportunity after you are hired. Being the newest, youngest, and least experienced will probably mean you will be asked to do projects and take responsibilities that may be below your abilities, or may not correspond to your interests. Try to treat each assignment as a learning experience and keep your ego out of the job.

Use your resources to their fullest potential. Take advantage of all the options available to you to learn in your current environment. In-house training, task forces, committees, and special projects might all be available to you—if you show you are interested. Learn all you can, as soon as you can, since you never know how long you will be there.

9 *The Most Common Job-Hunting Mistakes*

1. ***Not taking action.*** Putting off decisions, phone calls, leads, writing, looking. Not doing anything constructive. Avoiding even thinking about doing something. Making excuses, limiting yourself, erecting roadblocks to progress, complaining and generally procrastinating.

2. ***Not reflecting enough.*** Not thinking about what is wanted, ideal, or possible. Jumping to the search and jumping too often to the wrong job, simply because it appeared first.

3. ***Not taking advantage of all potential resources while searching.*** Overlooking the assistance and leads that can be found in talking with friends, parents, professors, etc. Not using libraries. Hesitating to call people unknown to you.

4. ***Not exploiting skills and experience.*** Not understanding the unique value, strengths and marketability of your past.

5. ***Not being committed to the job search.*** Not making adequate time for preparing and searching; not giving it the highest priority. Hoping something will turn up.

6. *Not empathizing with the employer's perspective.* The employer has needs, timeframes, problems and constraints that may or may not be compatible with yours.

7. *Not being positive.* Underestimating the power of attitude on the process, the employer, and you.

8. *Not anticipating and practicing for an interview.* Not being able to relate your abilities to the employer's needs. Not role-playing and formulating a strategy for success.

9. *Not following-up in a professional manner.* Thank-you letters, even after rejections, can make a name for you in what may prove to be a small, closely knit profession.

►These nine common mistakes are reflected in the following survey results and reported by employers.►

50 Reasons For Not Offering A Job

Below, in rank order, are reasons business and industrial managers gave for not offering a job to a new graduate, based upon a survey by Frank S. Endicott, former Director of Placement of Northwestern University.

1. Poor personal appearance.
2. Overbearing, know-it-all attitude.
3. Inability to express self clearly: poor voice, diction, grammer.
4. Lack of planning for career; no purpose or goals.
5. Lack of confidence and poise.
6. Lack of interest and enthusiasm.
7. Failure to participate in extracurricular activities.
8. Overemphasis on money: interested only in best dollar offer.
9. Poor scholastic record—just got by.
10. Unwilling to start at the bottom—expects too much, too soon.
11. Makes excuses, evasiveness, hedges on unfavorable factors in record.
12. Lack of tact.
13. Lack of maturity.
14. Lack of courtesy.
15. Condemnation of past employers.
16. Lack of social understandings.
17. Marked dislike for school work.
18. Lack of vitality
19. Fails to look interviewer in the eye.
20. Limp, fishy handshake.
21. Indecision.
22. Loafs during vacations preferring lakeside pleasures.
23. Unhappy married life.
24. Friction with parents.
25. Sloppy application.
26. Merely shopping around.
27. Only wants a job for short time.
28. Little sense of humor.
29. Lack of knowledge of field of specialization.
30. Parents make decisions for him.

31. No interest in company or industry.
32. Emphasis on who he knows.
33. Unwillingness to go where we will send him.
34. Cynical.
35. Low moral standards.
36. Lazy.
37. Intolerant with strong prejudices.
38. Narrow interests.
39. Spends much time at movies.
40. Poor handling of personal finances.
41. No interest in community activities.
42. Inability to take criticism.
43. Lack of appreciation for the value of experience.
44. Radical ideas.
45. Late to interview without good reason.
46. Never heard of company.
47. Failure to express appreciation for interviewer's time.
48. Asks no questions about the job.
49. High-pressure type.
50. Indefinite responses to questions.

When asked what would make college graduates more employable, responses included: get as much job experience as possible through co-op plans, internships or summer employment; develop communications skills—oral and written; keep grades up; take business related courses—especially technical courses, computer science and business administration; research companies thoroughly when making application; have clear purposes and goals; and know how to interview.

Appendix:
Additional Career Resources

Following are a variety of written materials taken from successful job-hunting campaigns. Choose the samples that best highlight your strengths and relevant experience for the job you seek.

Additional Job-Hunting Resources

Here are some of the very best books in the job-hunting and career planning field. In addition to all of the information from each of the authors (and these are the best) there is a wealth of resource material in each book that can be used to pursue particulars of just about any career that might be imagined.

Bolles, Richard N., *What Color Is Your Parachute?* Ten Speed Press, 1985, $8.95, paper. *The Three Boxes of Life*, Ten Speed Press, 1978, $9.95, paper. *The New Quick Job-Hunting Map*, Ten Speed Press, P.O. Box 7123, Berkeley, CA 94707, 1985, $2.95, paper.

Briggs, James, I., *The Berkeley Guide to Employment for New College Graduates*, Ten Speed Press, 1984, $7.95, paper.

Crystal, John, and Bolles, Richard N., *Where Do I Go From Here With My Life? The Crystal Life Planning Manual*, Ten Speed Press, 1974, $9.95, paper.

Figler, Howard E., *The Complete Job Search Handbook: Presenting the Skills You Need to Get Any Job, And Have A Good Time Doing It*, Holt, Rinehart and Winston, 383 Madison Avenue, New York, NY 10017, 1979, $5.95, paper. *Path: Career Workbook for Liberal Arts Students*, The Carroll Press Publishers, Box 8113, Cranston, RI 02920, 1979.

Germann, Richard, and Arnold, Peter, *Bernard Haldane Associates' Job and Career Building*, Ten Speed Press, 1981, 1979, $6.95, paper.

Haldane, Bernard, *How to Make a Habit of Success*, Acropolis Books, Ltd., 2400 17th Street, NW, Washington, DC 20009, 1960, $4.95, paper.

Haldane, Bernard, and Jean, and Martin, Lowell, *Job Power: The Young People's Job Finding Guide*, Acropolis Books, Ltd., 2400 17th Street, NW, Washington, DC 20009, $4.95, paper.

Haldane, Bernard, and Haldane, Jean M., *Job Finding Power*, Bernard Haldane, 4502 54th Avenue, NE, Seattle, WA 98105, 1984, $8.75, paper.

Holland, John, *Making Vocational Choices: A Theory of Careers*, Prentice-Hall, Inc., Englewood Cliffs, NJ 07632, 1973, $15.95, paper.

Irish, Richard K., *Go Hire Yourself An Employer*, Anchor Press, 245 Park Avenue, New York, NY 10167, 1978, 1973, $6.95, paper.

Jackson, Tom. *Guerilla Tactics in the Job Market* (revised), Bantam Books, 666 Fifth Avenue, New York, NY 10103, 1980, $3.95, paper.

Lathrop, Richard, *Don't Use a Resume*, Ten Speed Press, 1980, $1.95, paper. *Who's Hiring Who*, Ten Speed Press, 1977, $7.95, paper.

Medley, H. Anthony, *Sweaty Palms: The Neglected Art of Being Interviewed*, Ten Speed Press, 1984, 1978, $7.95, paper.

Parker, Yana, *Damn Good Resume Guide*, Ten Speed Press, 1984, $4.95, paper.

Government Documents

Here are recent government publications in the field. There are new publications and updated material constantly produced so check with the Office of the Superintendent of Documents and/or your local library for the most recent additions.

Available from the Superintendent of Documents, U.S. Government Printing Office, Washington, DC 20402 or from most libraries:

Dictionary of Occupational Titles
Occupational Outlook Handbook

Available at low cost from the Consumer Information Center, Department DD, Pueblo, CO 81009:

Occupations in Demand, #533J, free listing of job openings, revised monthly.

Matching Personal and Job Characteristics, #125J, 15pp, 1978.

Merchandising Your Job Talents, #208J, 24pp, 1980.

Starting and Managing a Small Business of Your Own, #129J, 95pp, 1978.

Study and Teaching Opportunities Abroad, #126J, 76pp, 1981.

Women's Handbook, #638J, 17pp, 1980.

Job Options for Women in the 80's, #201J, 28pp, 1980.

Sample Cover Letter

975 Wayne Street
Denver, CO   80598
547-4318

April 21, 198___

Mr. Wayne Adams
President
The Adams Company
1903 Hillside Avenue
Denver, CO 80603

◄ Address your letter to a specific individual — preferably, one you've had a chance to speak with.

Dear Mr. Adams:

When we spoke briefly on the telephone yesterday, I promised to send you additional information about my abilities and achievements.

In each of my work experiences I have focused attention on ways to increase worker productivity. For example, I helped to increase the turnaround time of work requests by 20 percent over a four-month period in my most recent position. At my suggestion, the work flow process was changed to allow for more flexible scheduling which resulted in a 40 percent decrease in tardiness. Other achievements are outlined for your review on the enclosed resume.

These illustrate the skills that I could bring to your company. I will call you later this week to see when we might be able to schedule a meeting to further discuss these and other issues.

Sincerely,

Sarah Smith Gilmore

Enclosure

Sample Cover Letter

97 South Larson Avenue
Philadelphia, PA   19709

March 21, 198___

Mrs. Margaret Johnson
Director
AIM Inc.
1344-22nd Avenue South
Washington, D.C.   20010

Dear Ms. Johnson:

As discussed, I will graduate in May of this year
from the University of Pennsylvania with a degree
in communications. I seek an opportunity to assist
a consulting firm while learning more about the
profession.

The consulting projects I have completed show my
willingness to accept responsibility. These
projects were successfully completed while I was
carrying a full academic schedule. My major has
helped to develop skills in organizational and
interpersonal communication.

I would very much like to speak with you or one of
your associates about future opportunities with
your firm. I will contact your office within a week
to see if this is possible. I have enclosed a copy of
my major plan and "Four Year Education Plan" to give
you a better idea of my abilities. Thank you for
your consideration and time.

Sincerely,

Tell them what follow-up you will do on your letter.

John Baker

Enclosures-3

Additional Materials

Other written materials (projects, articles, etc.) can be useful in the job hunt when used at an appropriate time (in an interview or with a thank-you letter). For example, following is a "Four-Year Education Plan" which served to help the job hunter organize and interrelate past experiences while providing additional relevant information to prospective employers.

◄ This is an option — it is a sample plan mentioned in the cover letter.

FOUR-YEAR EDUCATION PLAN

I chose Amherst College because I decided that I wanted personal, diversified education. I wanted a chance to develop the qualities within me that make me a unique individual. Consequently, I created my own educational structure that integrated my entire existence as a student: academic, co-curricular and personal life. In my last four years I have intertwined these three areas to become a full-time student of life.

One of my first courses as a freshman was a seminar entitled "Study of Lives" with the Director of Counseling and Psychological Services. In it we analyzed the lives of great and ordinary men and women of the past, and used the perspective that we gained to analyze and do some planning of our own lives. I developed my thoughts in an autobiography as part of the course.

One of the things that I learned was very important to me was communication. All of my experiences seemed to lead back to it. I had always been involved in activities that stressed meeting and dealing with numerous people. I have moved every four years of my life and each time I had to adjust to a new environment, new friends, and overcome new problems. Each summer I have been involved in an activity which gave me contact with thousands of people. The key to successful interaction in each case was the ability to communicate in the proper manner given the context of the situation. It is this ability that I have tried to further develop in the last four years.

Interpersonal communication skills I developed as a Youth Emergency Services counselor, helping people to understand and solve their personal and non-personal problems; as a Resident Assistant, helping students adjust and cope with a new environment; and as a motivational tutor, helping gifted elementary school students learn from new sources of stimuli. In the summer of 1976 I took a 5,000-mile cross-country bicycle trip during which I met thousands of people from different cultures and lifestyles. Effective interpersonal communication allowed me to obtain the most from these interactions.

I also worked on developing my organizational communication skills. I learned to organize and conduct a quickly moving group meeting and also how to effectively manage my time. I learned how to work within a formal bureaucracy (be it by petition process, judicial proceedings, or unwritten rules learned as a Student Housing Administrator) to achieve desired ends.

I have tried to apply concepts that I have learned in courses and seminars to generally improve the workings of the college. For example, the concept of accountability, which I considered in *Administrative Behavior*, I used to help reorganize the maintenance department of the college in 1976 . This included a relocation of supervisors and the writing of new job descriptions. In the summer of 1977, I used the concepts learned in *Organizational Communication* to reorganize the offices of the student union so that students would have easiest access to those offices that they needed the most. My proposal was adapted by the administration of the college. I later applied a communication analysis to the physical plant to develop a three-way system of feedback for work requests.

Research projects for academic courses included: "Capital Gains Taxation Loophole" for *Politics and Social Change*;"The Development of Monopoly Power in the U.S." for *Contemporary Legal Problems*; a cooperative project which developed a grant request to conduct a survey of higher education institutions for *Federal Social Policy*; a field study on helping behavior for *Social Psychology*; "The Effect of Non-verbal Communication in Group Decision Making" for *Small Group Communication*; and a sociological analysis of the social reality of being a book salesman and of biking for *Analysis of Society* (the latter article was published in two newspapers).

I then tried to apply my general abilities to specific projects in areas of need in order to improve my environment. I helped to organize the establishment of a 24-hour study area on campus, an option for a set tuition rate, and a review of the services offered by the Physical Education Department.

In this last project (fall 1977) I combined what I was learning in *Organizational/Interpersonal Communications, Public Administration*, and *Industrial Organizational Psychology* with my role in student government to undertake a cooperative and professional analysis of the physical education department of the college. This analysis included doing research on the history of the problems of the department through reading past department review reports, correspondence, and meeting minutes. I then discussed the state of the department in indepth interviews with college administrators (2–4 interviews each), the full-time Physical Education employees, and approximately 50 students. I coupled this information with that received from a 350-person survey, a departmental communications questionnaire, a cost-benefit analysis of the budget, and presented a three-series investigative report for the college newspaper. I also worked with an economics major, a faculty review committee, two outside consultants, and my three course professors. My efforts were capsulized in a 15-page report with recommendations which I presented to the president of the college.

I now seek an opportunity to continue to help and learn with an organization that can make a demanding use of my abilities. The career opportunity that I choose is important to me because I know that it will encompass all areas of my life. I will apply my energies both in further developing the skills of analysis, interaction and organization and in obtaining new skills to readily apply to the needs of the organization.

Sample Abbreviated Transcript

MAJOR CONCENTRATION PLAN

Name <u>BAKER,   JOHN   </u>
     last   first   middle

Expected Date of Graduation <u>   MAY 1978   </u>
                                 month   year

Directions: List the courses you plan to take to fulfill your major field requirements, including courses you have taken, courses you are now taking, and courses you plan to take in the future. (See the current catalog for departmental requirements.) Consult with your advisor and then obtain the signatures listed below.

MAJOR DEPARTMENT COURSES

Dept.	No. & Sect.	Course Title	Grade
POL	11	Politics and Social Change	A
POL	50	Contemporary Legal Problems	A
POL	57	Public Administration	A
POL	74	Federal Social Policy	A
POL	83	Administrative Behavior	A
SPE	32	Small Group Communication & Decision Making	B
SPE	37	Speech and Language in Human Affairs	A
SPE	38	Persuasion	B
SPE	40	Organizational/Interpersonal Communication	A
PSY	13	Study of Lives	A
PSY	50	Industrial Organizational Psychology	B
PSY	63	Social Psychology	A
PSY	73	Motivation, Emotion, and Conflict	A

Major _____ I.D.I.M. COMMUNICATIONS _____

Are you planning other major or core concentration?_____ _____
                                                   yes   no

If yes, please list _____
Are any courses listed below
used in your other concentrations?   _____ _____
                                                       yes   no

If yes, please list _____

MAJOR DEPARTMENT COURSES

Dept.	No. & Sect.	Course Title	Grade
SOC	20	Analysis of Society	A
SOC	72	Social Organiztion	A
ECN	11	Principles of Economics	A
HUM	26	Modern World	A
ENG	18	Critical Reading and Writing	A
PHIL	25	Ethics	B

Advisor's Signature _____
(Advisor must be in your Major Department—whoever signs will be
considered your offical advisor of record)

Dept. Chm. Signature _____

Sponsor's Signature (IDIM only) _____

Sponsor's Signature (IDIM only) _____

Educ. Dept. Chm. Signature _____
(if seeking teacher certification)

Type(s) of Certification—Elem ____   Sec ____   Kdgn ____   Nur ____

Sample Chronological Resume: Social Services

Use a chronological resume when your most recent experience relates to the position you want. ▶

NAME

ADDRESS   PHONE

PROFESSIONAL GOAL:

Entry-level position involved with community mental health.

◀ *Use a "Summary of Skills" to integrate a seemingly unrelated past.*

SUMMARY OF SKILLS:

Have had a variety of counseling-oriented experiences in which I developed a high degree of interpersonal skills with: individuals and groups, preschool to adult, special education and traditional educational, minority and international cultures, and private and public programs.

Place "Education" before "Experience" only if you have recently graduated. ◀

EDUCATION:

| | Florida State University | Tallahassee, FL |
| May 1979 | B.A. Psychology/Social Work, G.P.A.: Cumulative: 3.4; Major Concentration: 3.5 | |

Spring 1979   **Independent Study in Group Therapy**
Studied organization and leadership of different types of therapy groups. Led a therapy group using role playing and feedback mechanisms.

◀ *HIGHLIGHT JOB TITLES!*

EXPERIENCE:

Fall 1978   **Adult Rehabilitation Counselor**
Phoenix House   London, England
Led encounter groups; worked with other staff members developing and implementing individualized rehabilitation programs at this life-style rehabilitation center for ex-drug addicts.

Summer 1978   **Child Care Worker**
Edgewood Children's Center   St. Louis, MO

Supervised children ages 6–17; counseled, organized recreational activities at this residential treatment center for emotionally disturbed children.

Spring 1978   **Staff Counselor**
The Bridge   Louisville, KY

Counseling and group work with runaway teenagers; consultations with parents, school officials, probation officers, and other mental health workers relevant to my cases.

Fall 1977   **Resident Assistant**
Florida State University   Tallahassee, FL

Supervised a floor of a residence hall. Extensive peer counseling; developed and implemented programs to promote a responsible, harmonious living situation.

Fall 1976
Winter 1977   **Day Care Teacher**
West Seventh Family Center   Miami, FL

Assisted in the day care center for pre-schoolers. Organized activities to promote cognitive and motor skill development. Taught classes on parenting, helping parents to learn effective, healthy methods of child raising.

Summer 1976
1977, 1978   **Elementary Special Education**
Title I Summer School   St. Louis, MO

Taught first and fourth grade public school children who were two to eight months below grade level. Responsible for developing a curriculum for reading, math, and language. Worked with parents to develop, follow-up programs for the home.

RELATED EXPERIENCE

Have worked with other groups including the Navajo and Southern Cheyenne Indians, and poverty-stricken people of Missouri and Kentucky. Lived with a family and became involved with different cultures during a six-month visit to Europe.

REFERENCES:

Available upon request.

June 1979

Sample Chronological Resume: Arts

NAME
ADDRESS
PHONE

PROFESSIONAL OBJECTIVE:
An entry-level position in commercial or fine arts.

EDUCATION:
Oberlin College   Oberlin, Ohio   1976-1980
B.A., May 1980. Major: Studio Art with a strong emphasis on art history.
G.P.A.: Cumulative: 3.6; Major: 3.75.

Specialized Studies:
— Collective practice of rendering the head in painting and drawing, January 1980.
— Analysis of cartooning as an art form, focusing on the work of Saul Steinberg, spring 1979.
— Extensive overseas study of museums in Northern Europe, concentrating on their holding, administrations and impacts, January 1979.
— Independent analysis of "kitsch" art as found in St. Paul, fall 1978.
— Examination and practice of political and editorial cartooning, January 1977.

Cleveland Institute of Music   Cleveland, Ohio   1972-1976
Studied Classical and Jazz piano and participated in recitals. Prerequisited by seven years of private study, 1965–1972.

EXPERIENCE:
Oberlin College   Oberlin, Ohio   1979–1980
Teaching Assistant. Introductory college level art survey course. Responsible for instructing practical art theories; gave lectures, assignments, and led discussions.

Georgetown Leather Design   Washington, D.C.   1979
Department Supervisor. Included commissioned sales, accounting, cashier duties, and inventory control.

Oberlin College   Oberlin, Ohio   1979
Research Assistant. Located and applied appropriate slides and information for American art.

Morrison Company   Cleveland, Ohio   1978
Catalog Coordinator. Designed and coordinated with manufacturers entire production of skills and product catalog.

"Norfolk Island News"   Norfolk Island, South Pacific   1976
Art Editor. Responsible for all photographs and illustrations for
each edition, supervised page lay-out, participated in printing
and collating processes.

Hawken Day Camp   Lyndhurst, Ohio   1975
Counselor. Instructed art and gymnastics and assisted with music
and dance.

CO-CURRICULAR ACTIVITIES

Designed and produced artwork for various college functions,
1978–1980.

Organized and coached college's first field hockey team, 1978–
1980; and participated both as player and captain in intramural
sports teams, 1976–1980.

Representative to student government, 1976–1977.

PORTFOLIO AND REFERENCES AVAILABLE UPON REQUEST

February 1980

Sample Chronological Resume: Sciences

NAME

ADDRESS
HOME PHONE
ALTERNATIVE PHONE

PROFESSIONAL GOAL
A position in biology involving field work.

EDUCATION
M.S. Fisheries, 1981 — University of Washington, Seattle, WA.
Emphasized quantitative Fish Ecology. Knowledge of statistical applications and use of computer facilities.

B.S. Biological Sciences, 1978 — University of California, Irvine. Dean's Honor List; President's Council Grant; National Science Foundation Grant.

EXPERIENCE
RESEARCH ASSISTANT, **Fisheries Research Institute, University of Washington.** (June 1979 to June 1981). Completed my master's thesis on the predator-prey interactions between Arctic char and migrating juvenile sockeye salmon at Wood River, Alaska. Additional field work, involving the effects of lake fertilization, included the collection and processing of fishes using beach seine, townet, and fyke net operations, zooplankton sampling and identification, chlorophyll measurements, collection of insects and benthic organisms, enumeration of adult sockeye escapement, and estimation of spawning adult age composition by otolith collection.

SEASONAL AIDE. **California Department of Fish and Game.** (October 1978 to June 1979). Analyzed commercial catches of northern anchovy, Pacific mackerel, jack mackerel and sardine for length, weight, maturity and age composition.

- Estimated population size, distribution and age structure of the northern anchovy during a two-week cruise using acoustics and a midwater trawl.

- Investigated the food consumption of Pacific mackerel as a major predator of the northern anchovy.

- Experimented with a technique involving an underwater video camera to estimate the spawning biomass of market squid.

VOLUNTEER. **University of California and Bureau of Land Management.** (August 1978 to November 1978). Conducted a rodent survey as part of an Environmental Impact Statement for the acquisition of land as a University of California preserve.

◀ Valuable experience does not have to be full-time or paid!

LABORATORY ASSISTANT. **Department of Ecology and Evolutionary Biology, University of California, Irvine.** (June 1977 to June 1978). Performed macrophyte and invertebrate taxonomy in the field for a rocky intertidal baseline study of the Southern California Bight, assisted a macrophyte productivity study at San Clemente Island's untreated sewage outfall and tested purple sea urchin food preferences for macrophytes that differed by successional characteristics and the degree of thallus structure.

PUBLICATIONS

Perkins, D.J., B. N. Carlsen, R. H. Miller, C. M. Rofer, G. T. Ruggerone, M. F. Fredstrom and C. S. Wallace. 1981. *Effects of Groundwater Pumping on Natural Spring Communities in Owens Valley.* California Riparian Systems Conference. Proceedings. In Press.

Rogers, D. E., and G. T. Ruggerone. 1980. *The Study of Red Salmon in the Nushagak District.* Annual Report. FRI-UW-8019. University of Washington. 48 pp.

◀ Include activities only if they relate to your objective.

RELATED ACTIVITIES

Fishing, underwater photography, hiking and cross-country skiing.

November 1981

Sample Functional Resume

NAME
ADDRESS   PHONE

Objective	Entry-level position as an administrative assistant in personnel or a related staff profession.
Communication	Developed grant proposals for community organizations, research reports and journalistic writing for classes. Verbal one-on-one communication skill with peer counseling groups and as a member of faculty and staff selection committees.
Administration	Record-keeping skills developed in a small business and as an independent salesman. Helped design and implement new forms for maintenance records of a residence hall.
Public Relations	Served as a liaison between students and administration on campus issues. Developed and administrated advertising programs for various lectures and meetings on campus.

Employment

1978–81	**Resident Assistant** Utah State University, Logan, UT
summer 1979	**Grant Writer** Apex Housing Company, Dallas, TX
summer 1978	**Direct Sales** McPherson Lumber, Dallas, TX
summer 1977	**Staff Writer** *Utah Statesman*, Logan, UT

Education	B.A., Utah State University, Logan, UT Major: Political Science; Minor: Journalism GPA: 3.4/4.0

Related Experience	1978	Chair, Campus Programs Committee
	1977-79	Member, Student Selection Committee
	1977	Counselor, Peer Resources Center

May 1981

Sample Qualifications Brief

NAME
ADDRESS
PHONE

objective

Editing, writing or research with a publishing firm willing to give responsibility to a hard-working, reliable and creative writer.

education

Bachelor of Arts, SUNY, New York, 1981 Major: Journalism with mass media emphasis; Minor: English. Edited campus newspaper. Working knowledge of Spanish and French.

practical experience with all facets of newspaper production

As an intern with a prominent community newspaper, was able to observe and learn the responsibilities of newspaper production from paper purchasing to advertising sales. Helped generate and develop news and feature leads which expanded the scope of the newspaper and helped increase circulation by 20 percent over six months.

successful ability to work with wide variety of individuals

Served as a camp counselor in charge of programming for two successive summers. Supervised student work groups and was responsible for all public relations for the organization. Developed a new promotions brochure which helped attract a record number of applicants in 1978.

motivated self-starter and leader

Through co-curricular activities while in college, was able to recruit two volunteer groups for the support of community organizations. Initiated a community bulletin for one of these organizations that has since received funding for its continued publication.

analytical ability

Have an analytical ability to manage budgets and schedules that has been developed throughout my work experience. Implementation of innovative scheduling techniques led to savings exceeding $10,000 in my current position.

February 1982

Sample Combination Resume

Alter or combine resume formats to present your best features! ►

NAME

Current Address
Address
Phone

Permanent Address
Address
Phone

◄ *Use this to more specifically focus your related skills and experience.*

Career Goal:

To join in an aggressive campaign for organizational development, research, and promotion within an expanding communications or public affairs operation.

◄ *List skills first if jobs you've had might seem unrelated to your objective.*

Professional Skill Areas:

Public Representation/Communications—Community liaisonship; lobbying (registered); oral presentations to both large and small groups; interviewing, editing, creative writing, design and layout of printed materials; assessment of advanced communication systems; radio programming and broadcasting.

Sales/Marketing—Extensive experience in institutional marketing, consumer sales, account management, product analysis, and performance appraisal.

Administrative/Management—Managed the implementation of a comprehensive admissions program in seven states; materials acquisition and distribution; supervision of clerical staff and students; served as staff advisor to college fraternities.

Experience:

Public Affairs Consultant—Minnesota Private College Council, St. Paul, MN 44101. Initiated a comprehensive economic impact study for the state's 18 independent colleges, data retrieval and analysis, report writing, legislative advocacy, and project management (May 1981–December 1981).

Management Assistant and Research Consultant — Wisconsin Association of Independent Colleges and Universities, Madison, WI 53708. Part-time position in conjunction with graduate program. Primary responsibilities in public information and association relations (January 1981 – May 1981).

Assistant Director of Admissions (public relations liaison) — Occidental College, Los Angeles, CA 90041. Visited over 300 high schools in seven states, increased applications to the college from the East by 30 percent, designed office publications (June 1979 – July 1980).

Public Relations Management Trainee — Universities of San Francisco, San Francisco, CA 94117. Edited and designed university publications, recruited and counseled prospective students (June 1978 – June 1979).

Sales/Marketing Representative — Vick Chemical Company, subsidiary of Richardson-Merrill Inc., Wilton, CT. Sales-to-call ratio of 97 percent, completed 106 percent of contracts, sold over $150,000 worth of products (June 1977 – September 1977).

Student Sales Manager — Southwestern Publishers, Nashville, TN. Number 2 salesman in division, paid 75 percent of college costs out of earnings (Summers 1974 and 1975).

Education:

M.A. in **Public Affairs and Communications**, University of Wisconsin — Madison, Madison, WI. Program fellowship recipient GPA: 3.65 (August 1981).

B.A. in **Psychology and Social Relations**, Williams College, Williamstown, CT. Graduated cum laude (1978).

February 1982

Include the date you prepared ▶
the resume to avoid possible
confusion later.

Sample Targeted Resume

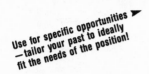

Use for specific opportunities
—tailor your past to ideally
fit the needs of the position!

NAME
ADDRESS
PHONE

Objective:
Junior Scientist liaison in a computer research facility between technical staff and non-technical employees or customers.

Capabilities:
- Ability to explain technical and mathematical ideas to non-mathematically oriented individuals.
- Working knowledge of FORTRAN and COBOL.
- Effective at quickly surveying possible approaches to software problems and identifying the best solutions.
- Clear and concise communicator—enjoy working with a variety of individuals in a service capacity.

Achievements:
- Received highest honors for thesis in applied linear programming, an integer optimization problem with applications to multi-commodity network flows.
- Decreased attrition rates of mathematics students by ten percent through initiation of new tutoring programs while in college.
- Streamlined organization bookkeeping procedures and financial records for a non-profit institution.

Education:
B.A., University of Michigan, 1979. Major: Mathematics with emphasis in computer science and statistics.

Work History:
1976–1979
   Mathematics Tutor   University of Michigan, Ann Arbor, MI
summer 1978
   Administrative Aide   AIM, Inc. Washington, D.C.
1977
   Assistant Manager   Baskin-Robbins, Bethesda, MD

June 1979

Sample Narrative Resume

97403 Peterson Avenue
Chicago, Illinois 70740
(312) 973-1400

October 12, 198___

Mr. Gary Cleavor, Jr.
Manager, Staywell Program
Control Data Corporation
1400-34th Avenue South
Bloomington, MN 55440

Mr. Gary Cleavor:

I am confident that my technical expertise and dedication to physical fitness can be combined to provide
an invaluable contribution to your staff.

◄ *Some placement professionals swear by this format! Letters seem to always get read, whereas resumes may only be glanced at.*

◄ *Include the most relevant highlights from your resume.*

As an Alpine ski instructor for over five years, I
have first-hand experience with the benefits and
difficulties of pursuing preventive health. As
part of my interest, I have written about the philosophy and techniques of teaching skiing.

In addition, my administrative experience as a management intern while attending Stevens Institute
of Technology has given me valuable insight into
the world of business and the practicalities of
office operations.

The relevance of this and other experience could be
further explained in a personal meeting at your
convenience. I will contact you shortly to see if
such a meeting could be arranged.

Sincerely,

Mark Schmidt

Sample Thank-You Letter

September 18, 198___

Mr. Henry Smith
Trainers Incorporated
2233 University Avenue
Berkeley, CA 94720

★ *Thank-you letters are important! They show interest and manners.*

Dear Mr. Smith:

I'm sorry that you were unable to keep our most recent appointment. Ms. Wilson met with me and gave me additional information about the position and the firm.

Tell them you want the job! ▼

I am still extremely interested in working for you. I feel the position would provide me excellent "grass roots" experience in learning how your firm operates and the problems you must overcome to achieve your objectives.

In considering this opportunity I have thought of some additional questions that I'd like to discuss with you. I feel that going over these questions would be a good start to understanding the responsibilities of the position.

Demonstrate your analytical abilities. ▼

◄ *PROJECT yourself into the position!*

- Has conisderation been given to using part-time trainers from industry or academia to broaden offerings at potential savings?

- Is training ever booked on-site at customer locations, allowing them to "host" the seminar and reduce expense?

- Are participants followed-up several months after attending to measure long-range impact?

Enclosed is an article that I thought you might find interesting. I look forward to meeting with you again and working with you soon.

Sincerely,

NAME, ADDRESS
PHONE NUMBER

Sample Thank-You Letter

June 30, 198___

Dr. R. F. Johnson
Corporate Technology Center
Hewlett-Packard Corporation
10701 Lyndale Avenue South
Houston, TX 77073

✦ This letter provoked an immediate offer when received!

Dear Dr. Johnson:

It is seldom that one comes upon an opportunity of such exciting motivational and professional dimensions as the position you described at Hewlett-Packard in our meeting of June 28. I perceived a strong team atmosphere in working to achieve corporate goals, with an emphasis on learning and individual development. It is the type of atmosphere that I would like to be a part of and contribute to.

I realize that I am currently experientially "green" to much of the day-to-day operational activities under your responsibility. But I hope that this does not cause you to overlook my potential in contributing to your goals.

I am extremely excited about this position. The people, functions and innovative environment all add up to making it an ideal place for me. I hope that you will not hesitate to contact me should you have any reservations of my not being a "match" with your organization.

I have taken the liberty to enclose a copy of my honors thesis on applied integer programming for your review. It should serve to illustrate some of the initiative I hope to bring to Hewlett-Packard.

Thank you for your time and consideration. I look forward to talking with you again.

Sincerely,

Provide additional examples of your work.

NAME, ADDRESS
PHONE NUMBER

cc:
NAMES OF OTHER INTERVIEWERS

About the Author

Robert B. Nelson is a freelance writer and consultant who has worked in personnel for several corporations and as a college recruiter for a Fortune 500 company. He has assisted numerous individuals in finding employment through his workshops, presentations, and individual counseling on job-hunting skills. He has an MBA from the University of California at Berkeley, and a degree in communications from Macalester College.

The author provides several related job-hunting services to readers, including: individual critique of resumes and cover letters (through the mail), related articles for publication, and presentations and workshops. For more information, or for comments and suggested revisions to this book, please write:

Robert B. Nelson
c/o Ten Speed Press
Box 7123
Berkeley, CA   94707

May we introduce other
Ten Speed Press books you may find useful . . .
over three million people have already.

What Color Is Your Parachute? by Richard N. Bolles
The Three Boxes of Life by Richard N. Bolles
Who's Hiring Who by Richard Lathrop
Bernard Haldane Associates' Job & Career Building
by Richard Germann and Peter Arnold
Finding a Job by Nathan H. Azrin, Ph.D., and Victoria Besalel
Finding Facts Fast by Alden Todd
Mail Order Moonlighting by Cecil Hoge
Bear's Guide to Non-Traditional College Degrees
by John Bear, Ph.D.
Computer Wimp by John Bear, Ph.D.
The Moosewood Cookbook by Mollie Katzen
The Enchanted Broccoli Forest by Mollie Katzen
Sailing the Farm by Ken Neumeyer
Write Right! by Jan Venolia
The Wellness Workbook
by Regina Sara Ryan and John W. Travis, M.D.
How to Grow More Vegetables by John Jeavons
Anybody's Bike Book by Tom Cuthbertson
Pleasure Packing by Robert S. Wood
Sweaty Palms by H. Anthony Medley
Finding Money For College by John Bear, Ph.D.

You will find them in your bookstore or library,
or you can send for our *free* catalog:

Ten Speed Press
P O Box 7123
Berkeley, California 94707